Ages 5-6
Key Stage 1

Gold Stars®

Supports the National Curriculum Key Stage 1

Maths

GW01179873

W0013920

PaRragon

Bath · New York · Singapore · Hong Kong · Cologne · Delhi
Melbourne · Amsterdam · Johannesburg · Shenzhen

Helping your child

⭐ The activities in this book will help your child to learn about maths. Pictures provide hints and clues to support your child's understanding.

⭐ Your child will gain the confidence to: count to 20, add and take away, identify a range of 2D and 3D shapes, begin to tell the time and order, group and measure objects.

⭐ Your child will learn about: numbers, shapes, halves, sets and pairs.

⭐ Set aside time to do the activities together. Do a little at a time so that your child enjoys learning.

⭐ Give lots of encouragement and praise. Use the gold stars as rewards and incentives.

⭐ The answers are on page 32.

Written by Peter Patilla
Educational Consultant: Christine Vaughan
Illustrated by Adam Linley
Cover illustrated by Simon Abbot

This edition published by Parragon in 2012

Parragon
Queen Street House
4 Queen Street
BATH, BA1 1HE, UK
www.parragon.com

ISBN 978-1-4454-7752-7

Printed in China

Contents

Write the numbers. Join each picture to the right number. Join each number to the right word.

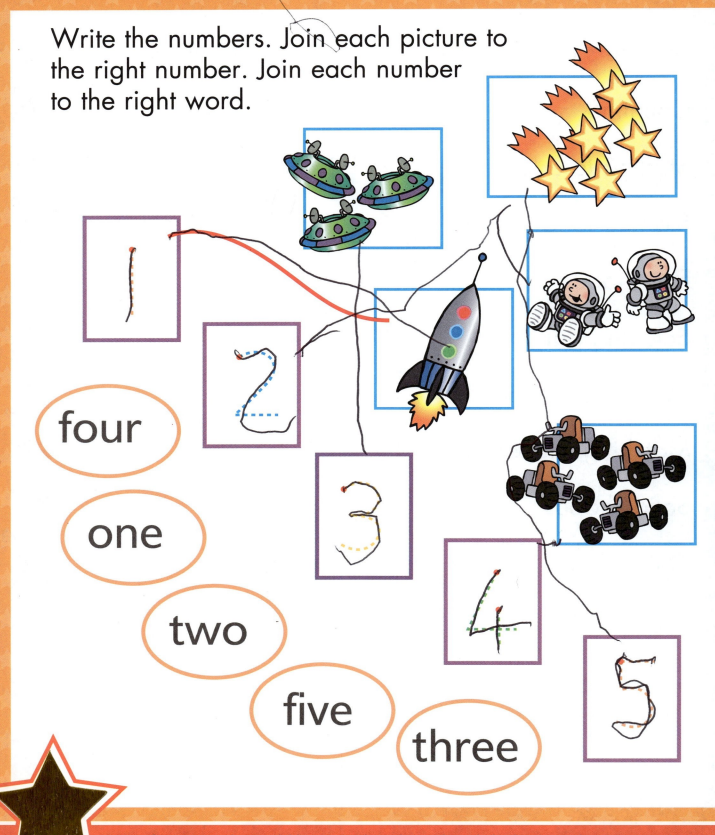

four

one

two

five

three

Note for parent: Ask your child to say each number and word aloud as he or she traces over them.

eight

ten

six

nine

seven

Note for parent: Help your child to work with numbers by saying a number and asking them what number is one more/less.

5

Count the spots on each dog.
Write the number in the box.

Join the frogs that have the
same number of spots.

Note for parent: This activity gives practice in using counting skills in different ways.

Each frog needs 10 spots.
Draw in the missing spots.

Join the pairs of dogs. Each pair must have a total of 10 spots.

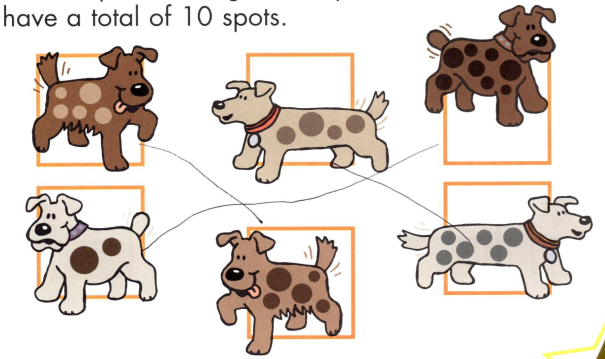

Note for parent: Help your child to write down all the pairs of numbers that add up to 10.

Write in the missing numbers.

 3 **and**  2 **make** 5 **altogether**

 2 **and**  4 **make** 6 **altogether**

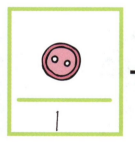 1 **+** 6 **=** 7

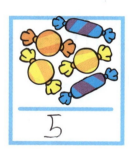 5 **+**  2 **=** 7

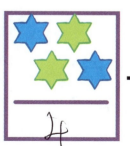 4 **+** 3 **=** 7

 6 **+**  3 **=** 9

Note for parent: In this activity your child is adding with objects, which helps to prepare them for adding with numbers.

Draw the missing socks above each arrow.

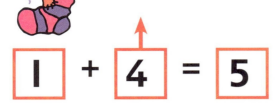

$$1 + 4 = 5$$

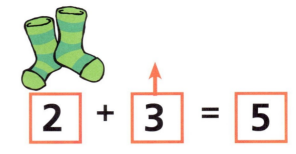

$$2 + 3 = 5$$

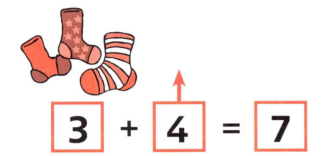

$$3 + 4 = 7$$

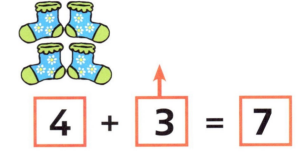

$$4 + 3 = 7$$

Write the missing numbers.

$$\boxed{} + 5 = 8$$

$$\boxed{} + 4 = 8$$

$$\boxed{} + 5 = 6$$

$$\boxed{} + 5 = 7$$

Dino the dinosaur eats 2 of everything he sees.
Cross out how many pieces of food Dino eats.
Write how many are left after Dino has eaten.

☐ take away **2**

leaves ☐

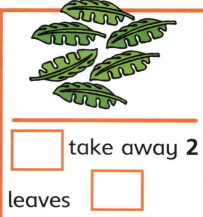

☐ take away **2**

leaves ☐

☐ take away **2**

leaves ☐

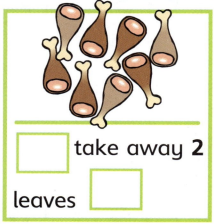

☐ take away **2**

leaves ☐

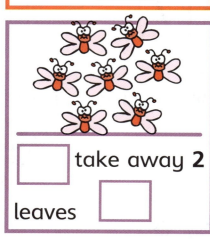

☐ take away **2**

leaves ☐

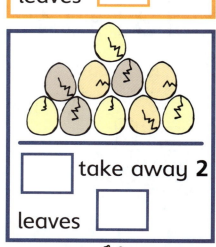

☐ take away **2**

leaves ☐

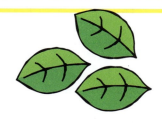

3 – 2 = ☐

2 – 2 = ☐

9 – 2 = ☐

How many fish has Charlie the cat eaten from each bowl? Join each START bowl to the correct FINISH bowl.

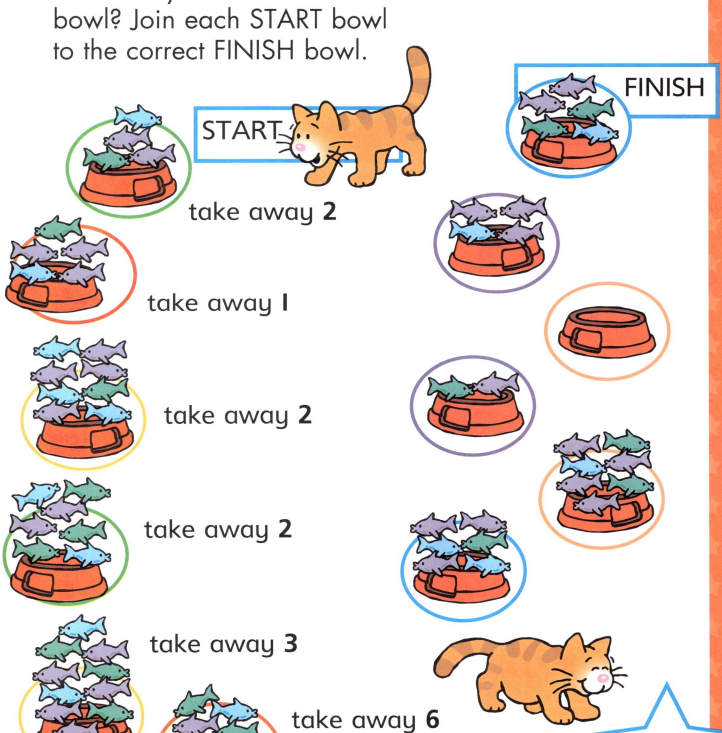

START

FINISH

take away **2**

take away **1**

take away **2**

take away **2**

take away **3**

take away **6**

Flat shapes

Cross the odd one out in each ring.

Tick all the shapes that are the same in each row.

Note for parent: Recognizing common shapes is a key part of maths teaching for your child at this age.

Join each set of shapes to its name.

circles

triangles

rectangles

squares

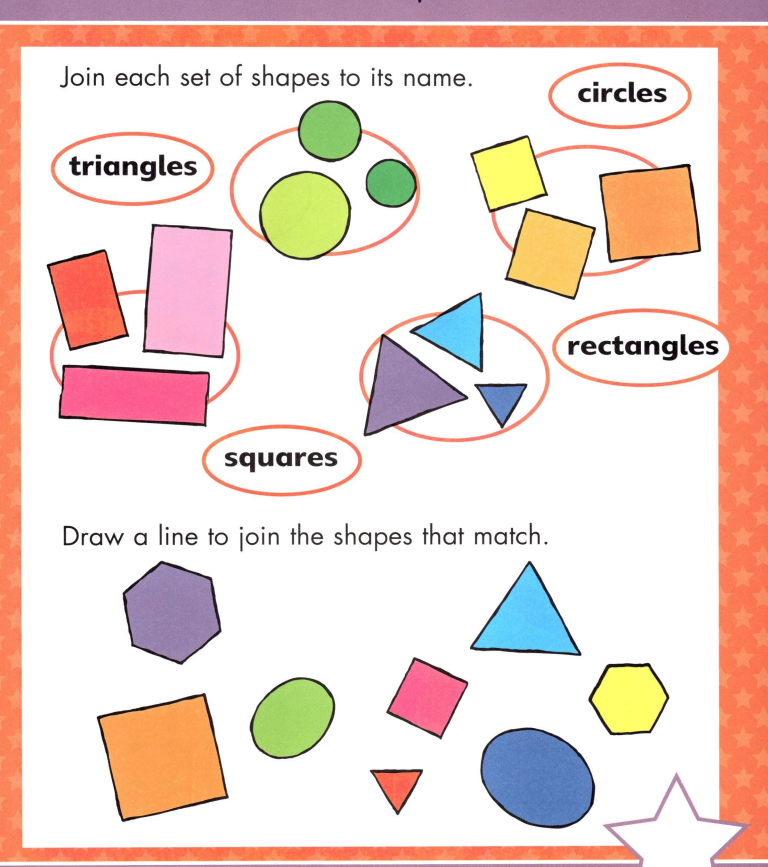

Draw a line to join the shapes that match.

Note for parent: Gradually your child should learn the names of common shapes.

13

Looking at shapes

Some of these foods are whole and some have been cut up into pieces. Join each whole to a cut-up piece.

Note for parent: This activity encourages your child to examine shapes closely. Ask your child if they can group the items by a different criterion – e.g. sweet or savoury, fruit or vegetable.

Matching shapes

Colour the matching shapes.

 colour red

 colour green

 colour blue

 colour orange

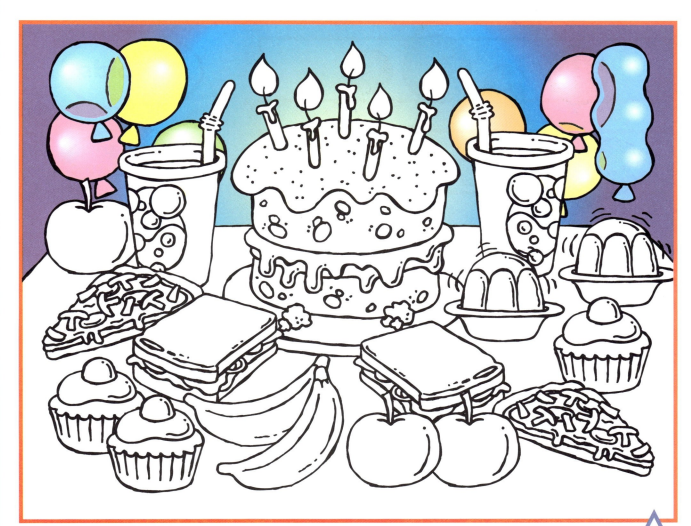

Note for parent: This activity gives further practice in examining shapes closely.

15

Solid shapes

Join each set of shapes to its name.

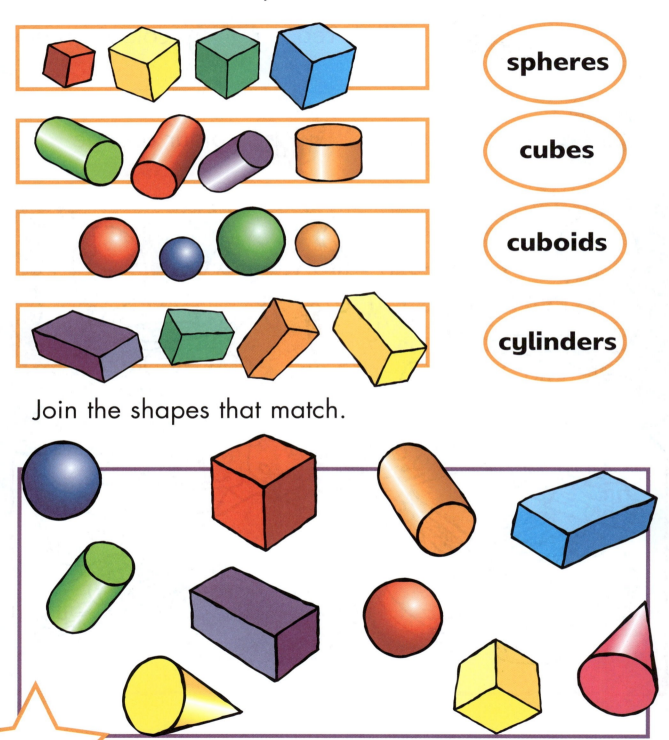

spheres

cubes

cuboids

cylinders

Join the shapes that match.

Note for parent: Ask your child to find examples of these solid shapes around the home. Ask them to recall the shape names as they become familiar to your child.

Join each START food to the correct FINISH food.

 **START**

add on **0**

 add on **3**

 add on **6**

 add on **6**

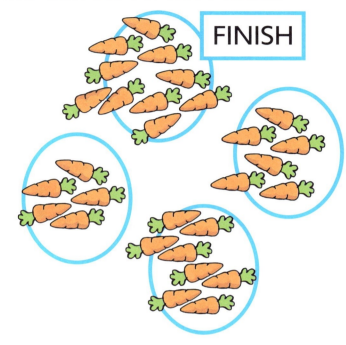 **FINISH**

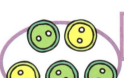 **START**

take away **3**

Join each START group to the correct FINISH group.

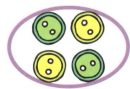 take away **2**

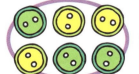 take away **0**

 take away **5**

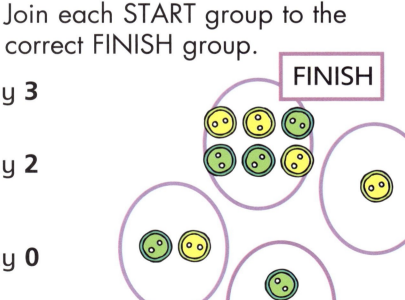 **FINISH**

Note for parent: This activity helps your child to remember about adding and taking away.

17

Colour half of each shape.

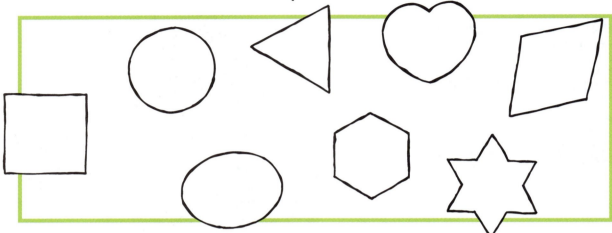

Draw the missing half of each shape.
Join the complete shape to its name.

triangle

circle

rectangle

square

Note for parent: Learning about half and fair shares is important in mathematics.

Colour half of the items in each container.

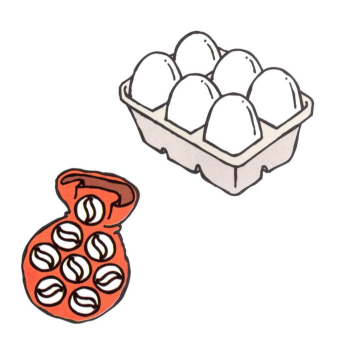

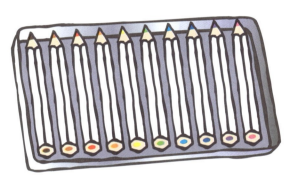

Some marbles are put into two bags.
Put a tick (✔) if the sharing is fair.
Put a cross (✘) if the sharing is not fair.

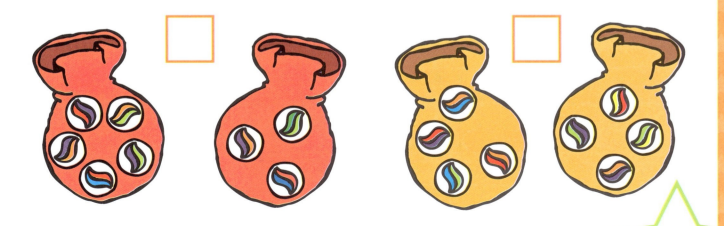

Note for parent: Encourage your child to practise sharing real-life objects equally. Sweets and coins of the same value are good examples to use.

Draw in the extra crayons.
Write the total number of crayons.

 1 add **4**

$1 + 4 =$

 **3** add **3**

$3 + 3 =$

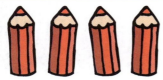 **4** add **6**

$4 + 6 =$

There should be 10 cherries on each plate. Draw the missing cherries.

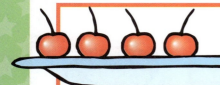

$4 + = 10$

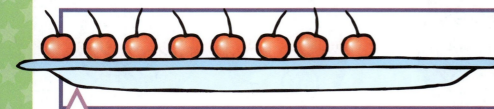

$8 + = 10$

Note for parent: Your child may need to use the number track on page 21
to complete these additions.

Use the number track to help you.
Write how many beads are on each necklace.

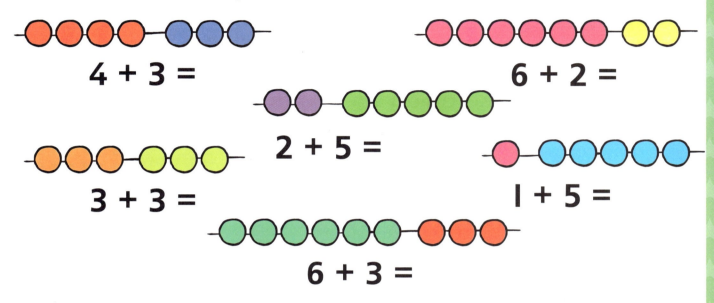

4 + 3 =

6 + 2 =

2 + 5 =

3 + 3 =

1 + 5 =

6 + 3 =

Join the scarves that have the same total.

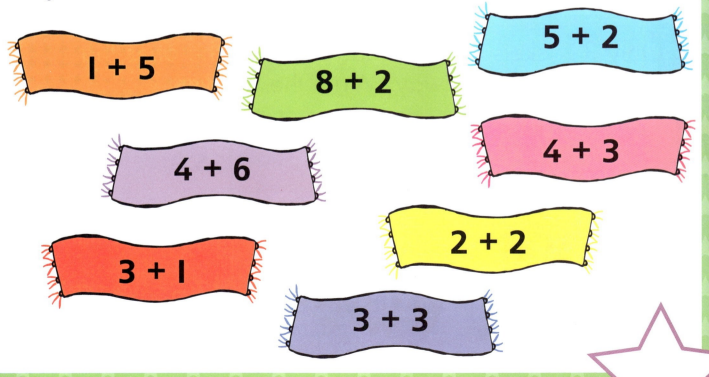

1 + 5

8 + 2

5 + 2

4 + 6

4 + 3

3 + 1

2 + 2

3 + 3

Cross off the animals to be taken away.
Write how many are left.

4 take away **2**

$4 - 2 =$

7 take away **3**

$7 - 3 =$

8 take away **5**

$8 - 5 =$

Only 3 rockets are needed. Cross off the ones that have to be taken away. Write the answer.

$5 - \quad = 3$

$7 - \quad = 3$

Use the number track to help you answer the subtractions.

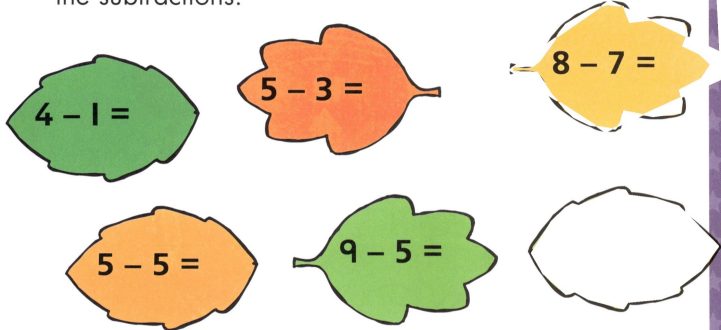

4 – 1 =

5 – 3 =

8 – 7 =

5 – 5 =

9 – 5 =

Join the stars that have the same answer.

10 – 5

8 – 7

5 – 0

10 – 7

6 – 3

6 – 5

23

Write in the missing numbers on the clock.

Write the times under each clock.

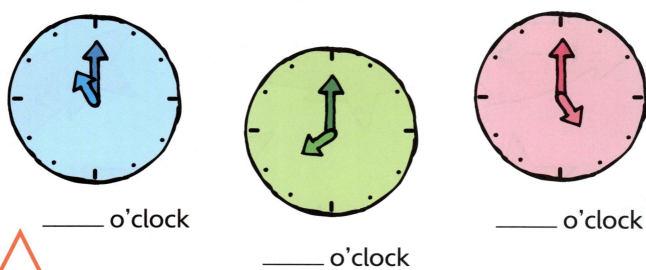

_____ o'clock

_____ o'clock

_____ o'clock

Note for parent: This activity will help your child to start recognizing simple times.

Look at the times. Draw in the missing hands.

half-past 3

half-past 8

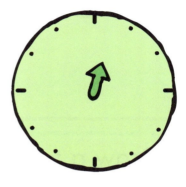

half-past 12

Write the times under each clock.

half-past _____

half-past _____

half-past _____

Note for parent: For further practice with the concept of time, ask your child if they can name the days of the week and the months of the year.

25

Measuring

Draw a longer worm.

Draw a bigger flower.

Draw a taller rocket.

Draw a shorter lamp post.

Join up the pictures in order of size.
Start with the smallest.

Note for parent: In this activity your child is learning to estimate and compare measurements.

Use the number track to help you write the answers.

0 1 2 3 4 5 6 7 8 9 10

$2 + 4 =$

$3 + 3 =$

$5 + 4 =$

$6 + 4 =$

$5 + 5 =$

$2 + 3 =$

$1 + 7 =$

$2 + 7 =$

$2 + 2 =$

$10 - 1 =$

$5 - 3 =$

$4 - 2 =$

$8 - 3 =$

$6 - 5 =$

$7 - 4 =$

$10 - 6 =$

$9 - 6 =$

$7 - 2 =$

Note for parent: Encourage children to look back through the book if they need help with the answers.

27

Write in the missing numbers.

Join each word to a number.

12 16

eleven   twenty

15   20

fourteen   sixteen

11   17

twelve   thirteen

fifteen   seventeen

14   13

Note for parent: This activity gives your child practice in counting to 20, and in recognizing numbers and words.

Join the dots in order.
Can you name the mystery animals?

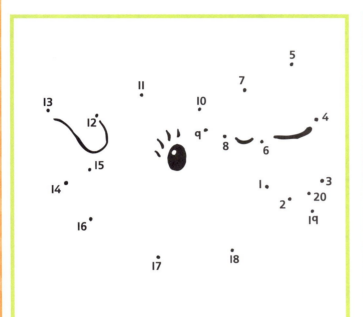

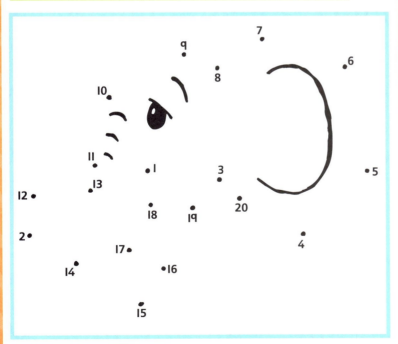

Use the number track to help you count on.
Join each monster to its correct answer on the track.

8 + 3

9 + 5

8 + 7

6 + 7

9 + 9

6 + 4

0 1 2 3 4 5 6 7 8 9 10 11 12 13 14 15 16 17 18 19 20

10 + 3

10 + 5

10 + 8

12 + 6

10 + 10

15 + 1

30

Note for parent: This activity will help your child to use a number track to count on and back.
Encourage your child to count on in twos and fives along the number track.

Use the number track to help you count back. Join each spaceship to its correct answer on the track.

12 – 8

12 – 6

13 – 4

11 – 9

16 – 8

12 – 5

0 1 2 3 4 5 6 7 8 9 10 11 12 13 14 15 16 17 18 19 20

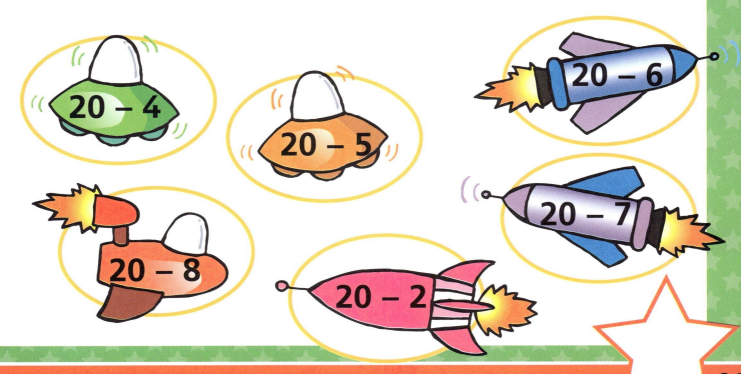

20 – 4

20 – 5

20 – 6

20 – 8

20 – 2

20 – 7

Note for parent: Encourage your child to count back in twos and fives along the number track.

31

Page 6

8 spots, 10 spots, 6 spots, 9 spots, 7 spots, 4 spots.

Page 7

Clockwise from left: 10 + 0 = 10 spots, 7 + 3 = 10 spots, 9 + 1 = 10 spots, 6 + 4 = 10 spots, 5 + 5 = 10 spots, 8 + 2 = 10 spots, 4 + 6 = 10 spots.

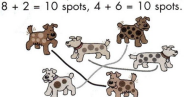

Page 8

3 and 2 make 5 altogether, 2 and 4 make 6 altogether.
Buttons: 1 + 6 = 7; stars: 4 + 3 = 7; sweets: 5 + 2 = 7; hearts: 6 + 3 = 9.

Page 9

3 + 5 = 8, 4 + 4 = 8, 1 + 5 = 6, 2 + 5 = 7.

Page 10

Row 1: 4 take away 2 leaves 2, 6 take away 2 leaves 4, 5 take away 2 leaves 3; row 2: 8 take away 2 leaves 6, 7 take away 2 leaves 5, 10 take away 2 leaves 8; row 3: 3 – 2 = 1, 2 – 2 = 0, 9 – 2 = 7.

Page 11

Page 12

Page 13

Rectangles, triangles, circles, squares.

Page 14

Page 16

Row 1 – cubes, row 2 – cylinders, row 3 – spheres, row 4 – cuboids.

Page 17

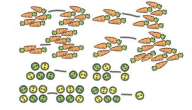

Page 18

△ triangle, ◯ circle, ▭ rectangle, ☐ square.

Page 19

Red bags = ✗; yellow bags = ✔.

Page 20

1 + 4 = 5, 3 + 3 = 6, 4 + 6 = 10.
4 + 6 = 10, 8 + 2 = 10.

Page 21

4 + 3 = 7, 2 + 5 = 7, 6 + 2 = 8, 3 + 3 = 6, 6 + 3 = 9, 1 + 5 = 6.
Total of 4: red and yellow scarves; total of 6: orange and dark-blue scarves; total of 7: pink and bright-blue scarves; total of 10: green and purple scarves.

Page 22

4 – 2 = 2, 7 – 3 = 4, 8 – 5 = 3, 5 – 2 = 3, 7 – 4 = 3.

Page 23

4 – 1 = 3, 5 – 3 = 2, 8 – 7 = 1, 5 – 5 = 0, 9 – 5 = 4, 10 – 2 = 8.
10 – 5 and 5 – 0; 8 – 7 and 6 – 5; 10 – 7 and 6 – 3.

Page 24

11 o'clock, 8 o'clock, 5 o'clock.

Page 25

From left to right: half-past 4, half-past 10, half-past 7.

Page 26

Page 27

2 + 4 = 6, 3 + 3 = 6, 5 + 4 = 9, 6 + 4 = 10, 5 + 5 = 10, 2 + 3 = 5, 1 + 7 = 8, 2 + 7 = 9, 2 + 2 = 4.
10 – 1 = 9, 5 – 3 = 2, 4 – 2 = 2, 8 – 3 = 5, 7 – 4 = 3, 6 – 5 = 1, 10 – 6 = 4, 9 – 6 = 3, 7 – 2 = 5.

Page 28

Top train: 9, 10, 11, 12, 13, 14, 15, 16, 17. Middle train: 11, 12, 13, 14, 15, 16, 17, 18, 19, 20. Bottom train: 7, 8, 9, 10, 11, 12, 13, 14, 15, 16.
Eleven – 11, fourteen – 14, twelve – 12, fifteen – 15, twenty – 20, sixteen – 16, thirteen – 13, seventeen – 17.

Page 29

Clockwise from top left: rhinoceros, tiger, monkey, elephant.

Page 30

8 + 3 = 11, 9 + 5 = 14, 8 + 7 = 15, 6 + 7 = 13, 9 + 9 = 18, 6 + 4 = 10.
10 + 3 = 13, 10 + 5 = 15, 10 + 8 = 18, 12 + 6 = 18, 10 + 10 = 20, 15 + 1 = 16.

Page 31

12 – 8 = 4, 12 – 6 = 6, 13 – 4 = 9, 11 – 9 = 2, 16 – 8 = 8, 12 – 5 = 7.
20 – 4 = 16, 20 – 5 = 15, 20 – 6 = 14, 20 – 8 = 12, 20 – 2 = 18, 20 – 7 = 13.